Credit Card Debt

How to Escape Credit Card Debt

Dermot Farrell

www.healbodymindandspirit.com

Dedicated to everyone who is sick and tired of living under the ominous shadow of credit card debt, and who would like to make a new start in life, if only they could find a way to do so!!!

TABLE OF CONTENTS

Foreword

I actually wrote this book back in 2012 and so the stats are slightly dated, but only slightly dated. It's difficult to get accurate details prior to around 2013, even now at this stage 2017, as it takes time for governments and organizations to assemble the financial details. The statistics in this book are accurate as of the year 2010 and any changes between 2010 and 2013 will see only minor changes in financial statistics. Furthermore while exact statistics will keep on changing over time, the general financial trend is towards a debt orientated culture and while the world is still recovering from the 2008 world economic crash and as such financial lenders are more restricted than they were before, never the less the trend is towards debt and the major focus of this book is to help you to learn how to get out of debt and more importantly to remain debt free, for life!

I wanted to put a lot of effort in this book to producing accurate statistics, as the statistics tell a story. The general trend dated back over a 50 year period, tells us that the financial system has become overly dependent upon a debt based society. The difficulties faced in rebuilding financial growth and stability, since the 2008 financial meltdown, stem I believe to the fact that the apparent economic growth of the 90's and early 00's, was largely based upon a financial debt bubble and that we need to move away from debt as a society, if we are to live a long and financially stable lifestyle.

While this book was actually written in 2012, but is now only being published for the first time in 2017, doesn't in anyway take away from the general debt trends and that we as individuals have to take charge and make some changes, as the financial institutions of the world gain both during booms and busts. During booms they get people to take out loans and during busts they repossess many items and sell them off thus making more money and gaining assets along the way!

Have you ever seen a poor Casino owner?

Probably not!

Have you ever seen a poor banker?

Probably not!

The thing is that the house always wins. The financial institutes have rigged the system so they win while we work hard to pay off our debts!

I hope if you read this book, that it will deter you from taking up debt in the first place and that you might even think about ways of bringing about debt reduction and a general life change, towards a safer and more long–term sustainable way of structuring your financial wellbeing!

Dermot Farrell

Hyderabad - India

January 2017

1. Credit Card Debt – the Dark Dide of the Moon

Looking at the stats!

Credit card debt has never been so high!

In early 2012, according to the e US Census abstract, there were 160, 000,000 credit card holders in the USA[1], that represents nearly 70%[2] of the adult population of America!

If we look even deeper into the figures, the picture becomes ever more intriguing. The average debt prediction for 2012, according to the Census Abstract, is $870,000,000,000. Now if we divide this by the figure of 160 million credit card debtors, the magical figure which it returns is an average debt per credit card holder in America of $5437.5!

The projected spending on these cards for 2012 comes to $ 2378,000,000,000, which suggests an average expenditure this year, per credit card holder, of $14,862.50! And the number of credit cards in America comes to 1,167,000,000 or 7.29 credit cards per credit card holder!

So we can conclude that 7 out of 10 Americans have credit cards; that on average they have 7 credit cards each; that they will spend approximately $14, 000 this year on their credit cards, and that they will retain approximately $5,000 in debt across all their credit cards at the end of the year!

Now if the average American is retaining $5437 on their credit cards, in the form of debt, that's a lot of interest, isn't it? And how about how many Americans are having difficulty with paying back this money each month?

According to Moody's April 2012 report3, while the credit card payment delinquency per month (that's the percentage of people who fail to pay their credit card debt in any given month) is on the way down, it still comes to 3.2%. That's 3.2% of 160,000,000 people, which is 51.2 million Americans, or 21 percent of the adult population of America, are having difficulty making payments on their credit card in the month of April in 2012!

And April 2012 is not an anomaly, the delinquency figures varies by a tiny margin from one month to another. So let's think about it, that's an enormous amount of people, ordinary people like you and me who are having financial problems. Remember credit cards are not in a vacuum, most people if they have credit card debt, probably have other debt problems too!

Indeed, if we look at the average bankruptcy figures, in 2011, they come to 1,410,653. Ok on the positive side its 11% less than 2010, which suggest that overall the economy is improving, which is a good thing. However, it still represents 0.59% of the entire adult population of America. That's just over half a percent of all adult Americans filed for bankruptcy in 2011!

What's your guess that most of them probably had some credit card debts in their debt portfolios?

Credit card companies and the credit card debt mountain

If the consumers are taking a hit because of credit card debt, then it is obvious that the turndown of 2008 has hit the credit card companies too!

Certainly the credit card industry has taken a hit. Back in 2007, the credit card industry of America had a bumper year with pre-tax profits in the order of $40.7 billion dollars, now that's a lot of money!

By 2009, however, the credit card companies had their worst year in 10 years, with a pretax profit of only $13.6 billion dollars. Fortunately for the credit card companies, the subsequent years, have fared a little bit better, with 2010 yielding $18.5 billion dollars. While the exact net profit figures on year 2011 returns are not yet available, the turnover for 2011 was down by about 5.5% on 2010 figures. However, so far in 2012, things appear to be improving once again!

So while my heart bleeds for the poor suffering credit card companies, after all they have had a severe setback, they have still managed to make profits throughout this global turndown. Bearing in mind that the 2008 turndown has turned out to be the next biggest thing after the great depression, it is still amazing that this industry manages to make, what are still fairly colossal profits, during what is invariably the worst financial turndown in the last 80 years!

So while the credit card companies have had happier days, they are none the less still profitable and well on the road back to recovery. Pity the same cannot be said of so many other industries!

Sadly the profitability, of credit card companies, is built upon the financial corpses of the ever suffering credit card debtors!

Just take a look at this graph showing the growth of the credit card industry between 1980 and the bumper year of 2007!

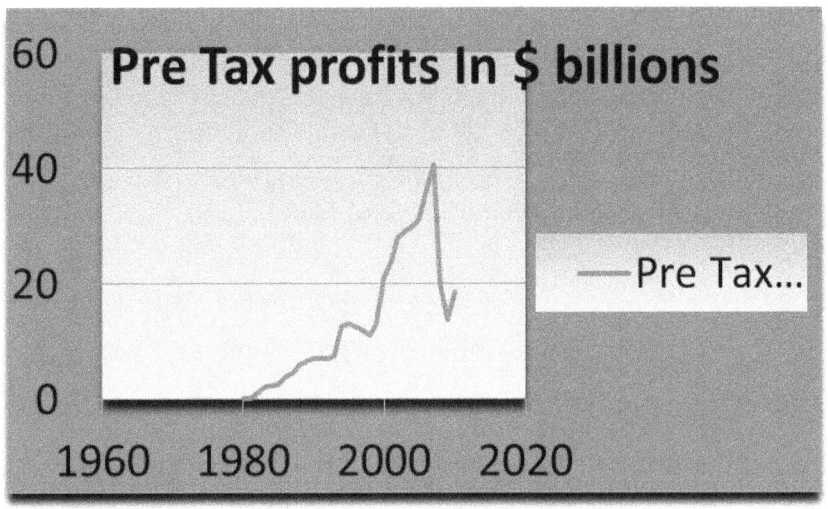

Even with an enormous downturn from 2008 onwards, they are still making money, and just look at the amazing exponential growth between the year 2000 and 2007, an increase from $12billion to $40.7billion dollars in a 7 year period!

And even with the 2008 downturn, while the profits drop from a veritable cliff, the credit card companies had obviously enjoyed amazing growth during this period, which was probably largely a result of the boom of the early 00's. So even with the reduced profitability, the credit card industries profitability is still quite amazing, especially considering that over the course of the last 5 years, large financial institutions, banks and even Countries have gone to the wall financially, whereas the good old reliable credit card industry is still making good profits!

Ok, so the credit card industry is still doing ok, how about the credit card debtor, how are they fairing today, and how well were they doing back in the great boom time of the late 90's and early 00's?

First off let's take a look at household debt:

CHART TWO MEDIAN VALUE OF DEBT FOR FAMILIES WITH HOLDINGS

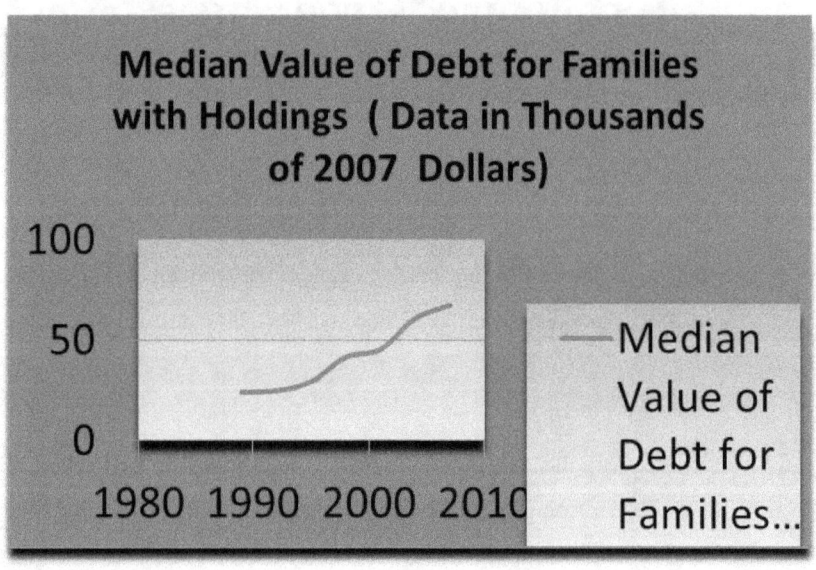

As we can see debt is creeping up on Joe Public since the early 80's. In particular this graph reveals the household debt as a proportion of disposable income. So back in 1989 the average household had debts which were equivalent to just over $27000 (by year 2007 equivalencies). Whereas by 2007 (remember when the credit card industry managed a new time high of $40.7billion dollars probability) the average debt in US households ran at just over $67,000, that's nearly a 250% increase in indebtedness over an 18 year timeframe!

This isn't simply a coincidence, the credit card companies and finance industry in general make more profit the greater the level of debt!

Since we are speaking specifically about credit card debt, just how well or badly has the American credit card debtor faired over the last 30 or so years?

Well let's take a look at the figures from 1980 to 2010:

CHART THREE DISPOSABLE INCOME COMPARED TO CREDIT CARD DEBT CHAINED IN 2005 DOLLARS

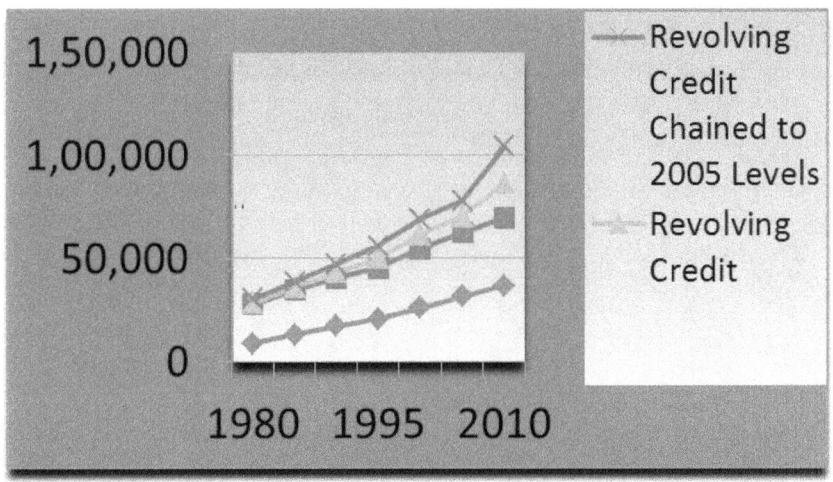

Ok first off the good news:

We can see looking at the blue line that disposable income has increased all the way along from 1980, without a break during this entire period. Even when we chain it to 2005 dollar figures (whereby the figures are adjusted to reflect year 2005 equivalencies) we see an upward rise in disposable earnings.

So, for example, in 1980 the average American had $ 8,794 in disposable income. Which when chained to 2005 dollar equivalents becomes $18,863. So the average American worker in 1980 had 18k worth of buying power, when compared to 2005 standard of living, after taking into account inflation over the years.

By the same token, in 2010 the disposable income figure had rising up to $36,697, which when brought into line with year 2005 figures, it becomes equivalent to $33,025. So the good news is that the average American has seen an increase in the level of disposable income by 75% over this 30 year period!

So this is a great step forward!

Now let's look at the bad news:

If we take a look at the green line we see the average household revolving credit, which back in 1980 was only $755 per indebted household. When brought up to 2005 equivalencies it becomes $ 1620, which is not too bad, as a percentage of disposable income it only represents just over 8.6%.

So how about taking a look at year 2000 debt figures. Well they were $6695, which by 2005 equivalencies becomes $7457. Ok an increase, but what the hell, even though it's a big increase of 460%, it's still alright. After all by the year 2000 the average American had an income of $ 25,944, which by 2005 standards would come to $28,899, which is a big increase on the 1980 figure of $18,863. So even with the increase in debt, the increase in income of income is just so much higher, that by the year 2000, the average American was considerably wealthier than their 1980 equivalent!

Now let's take a look at the 2010 debt level. It's a whopping great $ 16,383. Now when brought in line with 2005 levels, this becomes $18,204. This time the figure is increasing because of inflation, the debt would actually be bigger in comparison to figures taken from 5 years earlier.

Now this is an increase from the year 2000 figure by a whopping of $10747 per indebted household!

Let's put it this way, if we take the average indebted household in 1980 with $18,863 income (chained to 2005 levels) and $1620 in credit card debt, this means that they had disposable income of $17243 after we remove the revolving credit.

Now let's take a look at the debtor in 2010:

By 2005 levels, that average year 2010 disposable income of $36,697 reduces down to $33,025 in 2005 buying power. So if we take $18,863 from $33,025, what do we get?

What we get is $14162 in 2010 versus $17426 in disposable income for the average credit card indebted American from 1980!

This means that the average indebted American family in 1980 had a higher standard of living, 30 years ago, than they do today! And all of this is because of an exponential explosion in debt since the beginning of the new millennium!

Now I am positive that if we ran this same exercise across all debt, including home loans auto loans and so on the result would be even more dramatic. But even at this rate, the 2010 credit card debtor had just fewer than 18% less disposable income than their 1980 equivalent, because credit card debt had gotten so out of control!

Now take a quick peak again at the early graphs, which reveal the mind boggling exponential growth of credit card company profits from the year 2000 to 2007, and the similar rise both in household debt to disposable income ratios and the last graph which reveals the exponential rise in credit card debt. The figures are amazing aren't they!

It's one thing to argue, that perhaps the modern consumer based economy is a bad thing, as we can see from the 2001 figures; things were working out pretty well with the wealth of individual Americans. Even though debt was on the rise, it was way below the increase in disposable income.

So the present economic woes are really tied into the economic bubble which started in the 1990's, but which really got underway in the early 2000's. In particular the new global economy, whereby economic growth became unbridled, due to the ever increasing global marketplace, meant that the good times just keep on rolling in. This mixture of growth, combined with low interest rates, paved the way for good wage increases combined with friendly lending rates and special offers, which tantalized the debtors.

Of course 20:20 hindsight is always a luxury provided to those who look back into the past. We all know now that the financial boom which took place which was really no more than a bubble, which would burst with dramatic results. The negative moves towards higher rates of consumer debt over the last 30 years, would take a sudden euphoric surge forward and of course many people would end up getting bitten!

Just like the great depression, many economists and other economic gurus told us that we had nothing to fear, yet now we all know better. In reality back in 2008 the World economy became completely bankrupt!

Don't you feel it strange that 4 years on; things have hardly improved at all? That every time there is an improvement, almost immediately there is a financial regression?

Well mainstream media won't tell you this, because it would be seen as scaremongering, but the reality is that the World economy is actually bankrupt! However, rather than giving into hysteria, the powers that be, have made a concerted and necessary step of leaching out the losses over an extended period of time. If everyone had faced up to the harsh reality back in 2008, not one single economic marketplace would have survived intact!

So in many ways the global economy has been undergoing a mixture of debt consolidation and debt settlement, in an effort to correct the financial imbalance. Greece is the ideal and perfect example of this, whereby its debts have both had debt interest reduction (debt consolidation) and debt settlement (money wiped of off their debt slate!).

So we can easily see that the great boom of the early 2000's was really a financial fiasco which we are now (all of us in one way or another) undergoing the trauma of financial correction.

The good news is that the financial woes will finally come to an end, once all the outstanding debts are worked out of the World financial system!

Why am I talking about the World economy, when surely you want to learn how to reduce credit card debt?

Well there is no great difference between a Country and an individual, it's simply a matter of size. I am saying all this because, for a great many people, they feel anxious and uncertain about what is taking place in the World economy. So just see the World economy as a big version of all of us, and you will get the picture!

Returning to the credit card industry, it is quite obvious that they feasted well on the boom!

And even now with, the turndown, they are doing ok after all they simply increase their rates and off they go. There's no question about it the credit card industry is alive and well!

What can we learn from the 2008 downturn?

The first thing which we can learn is that the credit card companies and finance agencies will do just fine in the long run.

On a positive note, for the rest of us, even with all the negative spin surrounding the World economy, that the global economy will improve, even if it gets worse before it gets better!

While there are a great many negative points to be considered in a consumer based economy, the present financial meltdown is largely a result of over leveraged debt, during the period from the year 2000 to 2007. However, it will be resolved within the next two to three years. So don't going get distraught, the economy will improve, in the medium term, of two to five years! *

* This was my thinking at the time of writing this book, but now (2017) the world economy is still tottering, reveals a deeper truth about the world economy, that much of the growth between the early 1990's and mid 00's was in fact inflated and driven by debt, consequently the world economy is having difficulty in returning to these earlier levels of economic growth, as the growth was artificially inflated in the first place!

What is more worrying, than the state of the American finances, is the financial habits which have taken root in the economy. Credit card debt, and debt in general, were virtually non- existent 50 years ago, and even 30 years ago, it was quite low. However the finance industry and in particular the credit card industry is a behemoth. Even with the global turndown, it's an enormous industry!

The worrying thing with economics is that once big business, finds a new revenue source, it is very slow to give it up. Also all credit card companies belong to larger financial organizations, many of which have lost their shirts, as a consequence of the global downturn. Consequently many of these financial institutions see their credit card division as the last remaining profitable revenue center. So believe me, they have every intention of expanding their portfolios once again!

20

Hopefully the global financial bubble will not return all over again, however, if the credit card companies have their way they will do everything in their power to entice the general public into debt, because that's how they make money!

Hopefully the financial institutions will run more sober operations from now and on, and hopefully most consumers will be a little bit more conservative. But definitely the credit card industry will regain at least a little bit of its former glory.

The problem of course, as we see from the graphs above is that the credit card companies can only make a profit by impoverishing their customers!

Think about it this way. Running a credit card operation is a risky business. With the bare minimum of investigation they give an unknown quantity (their new credit card customer), a line of credit which is worth thousands of dollars. On a fairly regular basis these companies do get stung by credit card holders, who blow their cards and never make any repayments, so they have to leverage the credit card repayment structure in such a way that it makes high profit margins per customer, so as to make up for losses which they incur along the way.

Of course the high profits outlined above denote the success of their methodologies! But here's the thing, whether justified or not in charging so much to their customers, once you are signed up to a credit card, chances are that you will end up losing in the long run!

21

The dark side of the moon!

If like me, you like watching documentaries about space exploration, then you have almost certainly have heard about the dark side of the Moon. Basically because of the angle of the Moon to the Earth, we are always seeing only one face of the Moon. We never see the other side, which is referred to as the dark side of the Moon.

Well it's like this with the credit card industry too. On the surface they appear helpful, consumer orientated organizations, which help you (the customer) to go about your daily live with a little bit more comfort. After all credit cards are handy for making secure purchases, and indeed many of them even come with reward schemes attached.

However, there is a dark side to the credit card industry. On the dark side, hiding away behind finance industry waffle and spin, is the reality of debt which we have seen in the graphs above, whereby they profit from your debt!

In fact they have to profit from you debt, because as noted earlier, it's a risky business offering unsecured lines of credit. In order to cover the defaulters and make a decent profit, they have to charge outrageous interest rates and fees. So much so in fact that they will indebt you!

There are several factors which combine to make credit cards risky from the point of view of your financial wellbeing. In particular the two biggest factors are:

- Double digit interest rates
- Low monthly repayments

Double digit interest rates mean that whatever outstanding debt you have at the end of the month will quickly rack up in size. So even a small debt principle will quickly become a big debt!

Regarding **low minimum payments**; most credit card companies only look for 2% of the outstanding debt principle per month as minimum payments.

Furthermore, most of this small payment goes to service the interest on the loan. This is ok in the case of fixed length loans, such as home loans and auto loans, however, its pure poison when applied to credit card debt!

Put it this way, when you take out a home loan for the first 15 or 16 years of a 25 year home loan, the majority of the monthly repayment is going to service the interest, while the last 7 or 8 years goes mainly towards paying off the debt principle. However while this is fine with a fixed loan, in the case of a credit card it's disastrous.

For example, if you owe $1000 on your credit card and the card has a fairly high rate of interest, say a rate of 18%, with a minimum payment is $20 a month (2.0%); it will take 7 years and 10 months to clear the outstanding debt!

Interestingly, at the beginning only $5 is going to pay off the debt principle. As the debt is repaid, the proportion of money going to pay of the outstanding debt increases, so that near the end of the repayment term maybe $15 is going to pay off the debt and only $5 is going to service the interest on the loan.

Now bear in mind that the majority of credit card balances will take around 6 or 7 years to clear, so for the first few years at minimum payment levels you will be mainly paying off interest, while only in the last year or so will you be paying back the majority of the outstanding debt principle. However, in the real World, how many credit users create a balance of say $1,000, then make no more payments and instead they spend the next 7 or 8 years paying a monthly minimum payment of $20, each and every month, in order to clearing the debt?

Well, obviously not very many!

So what happens if next month you add another $100 to your credit card, just like most people do, then you are back at square one again. If you keep adding debt to the card, without clearing the outstanding debt principle, the majority of the payment will always go towards serving the interest!

Looking at minimum payments they tend to take at least 7 years to settle. So for example this $1000 debt, if it is at 12.78 %(the industry average (4)), will take 6 years to clear, and this is a very small credit card debt! Many credit card debts will run over significantly on periods of time.

And here is the thing, if you keep on adding purchases; you end up paying back the interest on the debt rather than the debt itself. So in the case of credit card debt payment structure, it is structured as if it were a fixed long repayment, even though it is a flexible loan!

It is this combination of double digit interest rates, which when combined with small minimum payments which quickly entrap the credit card debtor, so that even a small debt quickly racks up into a more significant debt!

In particular, it must be remembered that the credit card debt industry needs you (the credit card debtor), to get into debt and stay there, so that they can make a profit!

And every aspect of the credit card payments structure is designed to suck the debtor into a virtually unbreakable debt cycle. From the double digit interest rates to the low monthly minimum payments, from the exorbitant late fees and extra penalty interest rates which they charge, every aspect of the credit card industry is designed to create debt and keep their customers in a state of indebtedness.

After all this is the only way they can make money, they need some customers to become indebted in order to make up for those customers who default or defraud them!

Furthermore, after a taste of the mind boggling profits in the boom of the early 00's there is no question about it, the credit card industry will quickly reassert its market share!

Over the last few years, they have taken a hit. They have lost some customers and they have had to accept huge losses on credit card defaults, consolidations and settlements. Because of this maybe there has been less credit card offers, and more stringent guidelines regarding who they accept as customers and the kind of credit limits which re applied. But they are mounting a comeback and pretty soon the sweet deals will be back again!

So now that you know about the dark side of the Moon, what are you going to do about it?

Well the only reasonable thing to do is to see the credit card industry for what it is and make a concerted effort to become debt free and either stop using credit cards, or if you still use them at least make sure that stop racking up debts on them once you become debt free!

2. The Great Credit Card Debt Escape

So by now we can see that the credit card debt industry is insatiable. That they have experienced historical profits over the last ten years, and that once the economy begins to improve they will be back enticing consumers with easy introductory offers, is a certainty.

We also know that the credit card repayment cycle, with its double digit interest rates and low monthly payment structure, is designed to ensnare the unwary credit card user into a credit card debt cycle.

So if you are in credit card debt, what to do about it?

Basically considering the nature of the credit card industry, and the enticing repayment structure which credit cards offer, the single best option is to get rid of your credit cards and make a point of never using them ever again!

However, for many people this will be an unrealistic objective, because credit cards are just so useful in our present society. Simple activities, such as purchasing plane tickets for example, are difficult to achieve without the use of a credit card. Also so many merchants these days presume that the customer has a credit card, and the internet for example is designed around credit card transactions.

So for most consumers it makes sense to retain at least one credit card, however, it is quite clear that two things have to be achieved:

1) The debt has to be cleared.
2) The credit card debtor has to learn to use their remaining credit card(s), in a sensible manner.

So let's first take a quick look at the technical processes available which will help you to escape from credit card debt.

Credit card debt reduction strategies

There are two approaches to credit card debt reduction, which are namely do-it-yourself techniques and, for those who need it, the help of an external debt relief agency.

Do-It-yourself debt relief measures

These are by far the most commonly known debt relief strategies and include the old favorite tactic which is budgeting.

Budgeting requires the debtor to reduce their outgoings and redirect the money which they saved into paying off their credit cards. There are also variations on this theme, which can help the debtor, such as snowballing for instance, whereby the credit card debtor makes a tactical approach to paying off their credit cards.

So, with snowballing, the credit card debtor only pays off the minimum payments on all but one credit card, this one credit card receives the bulk of the monthly repayment. For example if the debtor has 5 credit cards, each with a minimum payment of $100, and they have $800 a month which they have put aside to clear their credit card debt, then they may pay off this minimum on four credit cards which comes to $400, and then pay off $600 on one credit card. Once this credit card debt is cleared, they then roll over this money (which in this case would be $600) onto the next credit card and so on down along, until the credit card debt is cleared completely. By snowballing the credit card repayments, the debt repayment time can usually be reduced by several months!

Budgeting is a great strategy to bring about credit card debt reduction. However the downsides of budgeting lie in its lack of leverage. Basically if you have a considerable debt, such as say $50,000, then it is unlikely that you will make much headway with clearing the debt, if you are only relying upon budgeting.

If we take this example of a credit card debt who has $50,000, in credit card debt across several credit cards with an average interest rate of say 14%, their monthly minimum payments will be in the order of $1000 a month, and if they only pay off minimum payments, it will take approximate 6 years and 4 months to clear off these credit card debts. And that's only it they make a point of not adding any new debts!

Now let's say the debtor carries out some budgeting and manages to put an extra $500 a month aside to clear the debt, it will still take them 3 years and 7 months to clear this debt, and once again that's only as long as the credit card debtor refrains from putting any new debts on their credit cards.

While it is possible to do this, it must be remembered that if a repayment plan goes on over a very long period of time, it becomes increasingly difficult to maintain the budgeting process. In the above example, if the credit card debtor has a considerable income say $100,000 a year, then maybe paying out $1500 a month will not be too big a cross to bear. However, if they are on an income of say $30,000 a year, which equates to $ 2500 a month, then even making a payment of $1000 a month will probably be an enormous burden for them. As for paying out $1500 a month over a protracted period of time, this will probably end up been an unbearable burden for them, and pretty soon they will end up giving up their budgeting program.

So if you want to escape from credit card debt, by all means do consider budgeting, however, also be realistic because whatever budgetary measures need to be taken, will have to be sustained over a medium to long time in order to clear the debt!

When the realities of debt repayment become a repressive burden, it is at this time that pursuing an external agency may well make sense for you.

External Debt Relief Help

Once the credit card debt problem starts to get out of hand, it's time to consider external credit card debt relief help. While you may well cringe at the prospect, it doesn't have to be as bad as you may think. Most things in life are frightening until we actually go ahead and do it. The same holds true to signing up with a debt relief company!

While we may not be happy with the state of our finances, there is absolutely no shame in admitting that we are out of our depth and in need of some external assistance. After all if we have a toothache we go to the dentist, and if we need to fix the plumbing in our home we call upon the plumber. Yet for some unknown reason many debtors feel embarrassed about their financial problems. It feels awkward to talk to a stranger about our financial misfortune, and many debtors make matters worse by not seeking help when really that's just what they most need.

Perhaps the reason why we tend to cringe at the prospect of discussing our financial misdealing's with anyone (let alone a stranger) is because there is a feeling of shame attached. Most of us have been raised to believe that people who cannot make ends meet, are either losers (as in they just couldn't be bothered to make ends meet) or they are charity cases (the sort of people who our parents or aunties or uncles would have helped out during difficult times). But never would we consider ourselves to end up in this boat!

So if your credit card debts are out of control, and you feel that budgeting is no longer working for you, then do consider getting help from an external debt relief agency. Forget about feeling embarrassed, getting yourself into financial difficulty is not nearly as unusual as you may think. As noted in the opening comments about bankruptcy, that some 1,410,653 Americans (approximately 0.59% of the adult population of America) filed for bankruptcy in 2011. These 1 in 220 adults filed for bankruptcy in 2011!

So if a few thousand people live in your neighborhood, chances are that a few of them have filed for bankruptcy in the near past. And remember that people who file for bankruptcy tend to have particularly serious debt problems. So for every debtor who files for bankruptcy, there are a great many other individuals who are undergoing serious debt problems, but whose financial problems are not so severe that they need to file for bankruptcy!

Also having debt problems is not just a problem for the poor; while low income families are more likely to undergo financial troubles, because of their low income, many middle income and even higher income families run into financial troubles. Usually people with a higher level of income end up in severe debt either through long term overspending (whereby they are living in denial regarding their overspending) or when they undergo a sudden turndown in income (as in losing a job due to the economy or ill health for instance). Sadly in the case of higher income debtors, who lose their jobs, they often dive very quickly into debt because their lifestyle is quite expensive and effectively eats up many thousands of dollars per month!

So get over the embarrassment and do remember that a great many people have financial troubles. It's only natural that they will try to conceal their difficulties, so while you may feel like you are the only person whom you know who has financial difficulties, then think again, you probably do know people with financial difficulties, it's just that they are not telling you. Let's face it not many people out there who will say "Hi there, how are you today, by the way I am hopelessly in debt and don't know what to do about it!"

Ok so we all know one or two people who are that direct, but do remember that for every one person like this, there are many dozens who will not come forward at all!

Next let's consider the terrible 'B' word, as in B for bankruptcy. Bankruptcy isn't such a bad thing, and it must be remembered that bankruptcy is a last resort. So let's take a quick overview of the last resort option first and get it over and done with.

Bankruptcy:

Bankruptcy is disliked by the masses primarily because it is so public, after all it's on public record and it involves a visit to the local courthouse. Also it wrecks your credit rating from 8 to 10 years and usually it results in a fire sale of most if not all of your assets.

Following court procedures the creditors contact the bankruptcy trustee, and then the trustee disperses the assets accordingly. Because the trustees' role is to wind up the bankruptcy, quickly and efficiently, their main aim is to disperse assets quickly. This means fire sale of assets!

However, on the good side at least it's a very quick process. It's usually all over and done with in less than 6 months, and although there is a public record of the bankruptcy and your credit rating is mangled, at least you are free of the burden of debt!

Basically bankruptcy is very good if you have no other option left open to you. However, fortunately there are two other options open to you!

Credit card debt consolidation: Credit card debt consolidation, works well for debtors whose finances are getting out of control, but who could make good on their repayments if they could reduce their monthly repayments. An example of this would be a credit card debtor with $50,000 in debt, and who has to pay out $1000 per month in minimum payments, but who can only manage to pay out $800 a month.

With credit card debt consolidation, the credit card debtor signs up with a debt relief agency that negotiates with the creditors on behalf of their client. They negotiate, to lower interest rates and fees, so in the above example a $1000 a month repayment may well be reduced to $500 or $600 per month, because the interest rates have been lowered so much. This provides the credit card debtor with the possibility of making repayments and possibly even making some more progress with paying off the debt principle.

Credit card debt consolidation, works very well with debtors who could regain control of their finances, once their interest rates had been reduced. By signing up with a debt relief agency, for a small monthly fee, they will arrange this for you.

Another benefit of credit card debt consolidation is that debtors credit score is untouched because the debt principle remains intact!

So what are the downsides?

36

Basically, credit card debt consolidation will not work very well for debtors whose credit card debts are seriously out of control.

So again if we look at the example of the credit card debtor, who has $50,000 of debt on their credit cards and who has to pay back $1000 per month in minimum payments. If they have a disposable income after expenses each month of $800, then reducing the monthly repayments by a few hundred dollars per month is a real lifesaver!

However, what about a debtor whose disposable income, after all expenses and after budgeting is only $200 a month, then even with reduced interest rates they will still be unable to make those repayments! In this case, most debtors will simply pursue bankruptcy. However, there is another option, which has less negative downsides and it is credit card debt settlement.

Credit card debt settlement: With credit card debt settlement, the debtor signs up to a debt relief company, then they stop making payments to their various creditors. Instead they put the money, which would have gone to service their minimum payments, into a special bank account. Once the amount of money in this account reaches approximately 50% of the outstanding debt principle, the debt relief company begins to negotiate on behalf of the credit card debtor.

Because they have not paid their creditors in a while, most creditors will be more than happy to discount the outstanding debt, just so that they will receive some money from the debtor in a one off settlement. Because of the aggressive nature of this debt relief strategy, the debtor can often see reductions in the order of between 40% and 60% of the outstanding debt. So it would be quite commonplace for a credit card debtor with $50,000 worth of debt on their credit cards see a reduction of $25,000 from their debts!

So in practice credit card debt settlement has some serious advantages over and above debt consolidation. Because unlike debt consolidation, with debt settlement, the debt principle is usually halved, so no need to pay 50 k when you can pay 25 k instead. Also, it has the benefit of brevity, because most debt consolidation processes (also known as Debt management plans or DMP for short) will take several years to clear off the debt principle, whereas with debt settlement all debts are usually cleared within the period of approximately one year.

Finally, it also boasts some advantages over and above bankruptcy. For example, while credit card debt settlement will result in a downgrading of credit rating, it will not be downgraded for such a long time as would be the case with bankruptcy. Furthermore, unlike bankruptcy, debt settlement is not on public record, and finally because you are in charge of the process, instead of a bankruptcy trustee, as in the case of bankruptcy, if you have to sell of some assets, at least you will not have to fire sale them!

As noted earlier the bankruptcy trustees simply want to wind up the process, consequently they are not concerned about getting a great deal. So for example, if you own a car with a market value of $20,000, the bankruptcy trustee may sell it for as little as $5000, if there are no other takers. And with bankruptcy, all potential buyers are looking for a bargain!

Whereas if you sign up to a debt settlement program, no one knows what you are broke, so for a start you will get a better type of buyer, and secondly you will be more likely to drive a hard bargain, because it's your assets which you are trying to sell and not someone else's!

So with the example of the car worth 20k, a bankruptcy trustee may only manage to return 5k, whereas if the debtor sells it themselves, maybe they will get $15000. Now multiply this by all the various assets at your disposal, and it is easy to see that with credit card debt settlement, that the debtor has a much better chance to save at least some of their assets!

So on the face of it credit card debt settlement sounds superb!

However, do bear in mind that credit card debt settlement is a very aggressive strategy and as such it does come with some downsides. For a start, unlike bankruptcy, your creditors are not bound by a legal agreement. So while many creditors will accept negotiations terms, some may not, and they may even bring you to court!

Another negative, with credit card debt settlement, is the downgrading of the credit score which is something which will more than likely not happen with debt consolidation.

And finally, any monies which have been reduced are potentially applicable for income tax once the amount succeeds $600, unless you can prove that you are destitute which may not be so easy to do.

So in summary, credit card debt settlement is a serious alternative to bankruptcy, however, for most debtors, who have less severe debt problems and who may have been considering debt consolidation, may well be happier to take this more conservative route, simply because it comes with a lot less hassle!

Basically debt settlement does come with some hassle; however, it comes along with far less grief than would be experienced by filing for bankruptcy!

In the vast majority of cases most bankruptcy cases would do better to sign up to a debt settlement program. It might frustrate your creditors, but at the end of the day it will save you money!

So if you have assets at your disposal or if you have a significant income, then debt settlement is certainly worth pursuing. However, what if you have few assets at their disposal, and possibly little or no income?

In this case, bankruptcy will probably be the better option for you. For example, in the case of the credit card debtor with $50000 in debts, even if they save $25,000 with a debt settlement, they will still have to stump up 25k for the settlement. Furthermore, they will probably have to make a tax payment to the Inland Revenue service as well.

Now if you have say $100,000 worth of assets, then this might make a lot of sense, especially if you consider that a bankruptcy trustee might get a very small sum of money for all the assets, leaving you completely asset stripped at the end of the process. Whereas with debt settlement you might get away with selling off only a small amount of your assets to make good on the 35k and taxes.

However, if you have no assets and little or no income, and you have a debt of $50000 well then debt settlement will not work for you. Why? Because how will you ever raise the 25k in the first place?

It's at times like these that it is necessary to simply accept the reality of the situation, and do what needs to be done, which in these circumstances entails filing for bankruptcy!

The most important point to bear in mind with all debt relief strategies is that each strategy suits a particular set of circumstances. The second biggest mistake, which is often made, is to simply follow the example of someone you know without considering your particular circumstances. Their debt relief strategy may well work for you, however, do some math first with your specific requirements and do make sure that it suits your needs.

The good news is that there is enough versatility, in terms of debt relief options, to find a strategy which will suit your needs. So do take the time out to do some research, into the range of services on offer, and then carry out a little bit of soul searching in order to see which the best way is forward for you.

I just mentioned that the second biggest mistake, which credit card debtors make, is by simply following someone they know without any consideration of their unique circumstances. Of course, in some case debtors simply sign up to the first advertisement which they come across, either way is a bad decision. So if this is the second biggest mistake which debtors take, then what is the first one?

Well the first one is to stick your head in the sand, like an Ostrich, and make no decision at all!

Even if you make mistakes along the way, do take some action, because if you delay, what happens? I'll tell you what happens, the debt racks up and a big problem becomes an even bigger problem!

As noted earlier, it can be difficult to accept the reality of our circumstances; depending upon our upbringing, we may even feel ashamed of ourselves. Well, let go of all such judgmental attitudes and instead make a concerted effort to sort out your debt issues. And remember that it's quite a common thing to face financial difficulties and debts!

Just because you don't personally know anyone with a debt problem does not mean that you are the only person in your neighborhood, or amongst your friends and family with a debt problem. Most people are really private about this kind of thing!

So do not make the number one mistake, amongst credit card debtors, which is to live in denial just hoping for the debt to miraculously disappear. So instead make a commitment, today, to resolve your debts once and for all!

3. Sustaining the Great Credit Card Debt Escape!

While it is easy to become entangled in a web of credit card debts, getting out of debt is a far more difficult thing to achieve. However, once the debtor takes the time out to study their particular circumstances and the various debt relief options available to them, it is possible to escape from credit card debt, so long as the debtor is consistent in their efforts.

However, a far more difficult achievement is to remain debt free!

While this is true of all forms of debt, in particular, it is true of credit card debt. This is particularly the case with credit card debt, because the credit card debt repayment cycle is intended to catch the unwary into a debt cycle, which is difficult to escape from.

If you want to escape from credit card debt, and to remain debt free, then it is simply not enough to follow the traditional advice which is aimed at relieving you of your outstanding debts. The problem is that the very fabric of society itself, combined with innate flaws in human nature, help to recreate circumstances which will bring you back into the debt cycle all over again. So prior to launching a debt relief strategy, do please consider the following points, as they will help you to maintain your debt free state, once the state of indebtedness has been eliminated!

The two factors which will draw you back into credit card debt all over again, and how to deal with them!

There are two factors at play here. The first one is a societal factor and the second one is a flaw in human nature. These two factors are:

- The 'buy today and payback tomorrow' consumer culture
- Denial

THE FIRST FACTOR OF 'BUYING TODAY AND PAYING BACK TOMORROW' IS A FEATURE OF OUR MODERN CONSUMERIST CULTURE

Between the year 1900 and the year 2000, the overall wealth of the World increased nearly tenfold (5), and the main reason for this was because of a rise in consumer expenditure. While it is a good in a way that there is more consumerism, simply because it increases all our earnings, it also had a fairly negative downside, which is consumer debt. As you can note by looking back at the second chart, on US domestic indebtedness since 1980, the average household debt has been rising exponentially.

While this is good in an emerging marketplace, because it stimulates growth, there comes a time when the level of debt becomes disproportionate to the level of income. Certainly over the last 30 or 40 years, there has been a disconcerting move towards this disparity become income and debt. Sadly because the World economy has been growing at a furious rate over the last 50 or so years (barring a few recessions), the World has never before seen such an explosion in economic growth, and while growth is good, in this case the growth hid the debt!

It is this sudden growth which has attracted the finance industry into expanding their consumer portfolio's. Because while there has been a certain level of economic turbulence, over the last 50 years, the general movement has been upwards. This means that finance companies can increase their consumer loan market, and still manage to get paid more often than not, because most consumers have seen, on average, an increase in their income figures over the last few decades.

Business, been what it is, is always endeavoring to expand into new markets, and to deepen market share in existing ones. As a consequence of this the finance companies have expanded their interests into all sorts of consumer based finance packages. Just walk into any store these days and everything has a finance package if you want it. And of course home loans, auto loans and bank overdrafts have also expanded their market share along the way.

Finally, over the last 30 or so years, the credit card industry has reached ever higher levels of market penetration. Back in the early 80's possessing a gold card was a sign that you had arrived, whereas by the early 00's receiving a gold card was simple a step along the ladder towards ever bigger credit card limits.

What happened in the late 90's and early 00's was an enormous feast upon consumer spending which had simply hit saturation point. The feeding frenzy during this period (especially between the years 2000 and 2007) was a direct result of the internet and the all new global economy. For the first time in the history of the World, it was possible to buy and sell anything from anywhere in the World to anywhere in the World. And while it acted like a turbocharger to the World economy, it also acted just like an acetylene torch on the already overstretched consumer finance market. With mind boggling economic growth rates, low interest rates, and finance company wizards working out the most efficient way to box off bad debts, everything was looking rosy in the garden!

That is until in 2008 the market bubble blew up in everyone's face!

Again referring back to graph one, on the growth of the credit card industry, it is safe to say that the move towards a consumer based economy had reached ever new spectacular heights in the early 00's, which were driven not by genuine economic growth factors, but rather by a frenzy of consumer greed and finance company recklessness!

Returning to the concepts of increasing consumerism, over the last 50 years or so, when coming from a low ebb finance is good. For example, if you have to pay for your car by cash, how many people would ever decide to buy a new, or nearly new, car?

Of course, the answer is not a lot. So, obviously a certain amount of consumer finance, at affordable rates of interest, is a good thing for the economy. The car buyer gets there car, which may well be necessary so that they can commute to work. The car salesman, car dealership and car manufacturers make their profits, and a thousand and one other people along the way receive some money out of the process of building, selling and maintaining that car on the road.

However, once the level of indebtedness turns into an enormous burden, it is at this stage that indebtedness starts to become a noose around our necks. Since 1980, the level of consumer indebtedness has begun to get out of control. Because of the exponential growth in the World economy, however, this move towards a debt imbalance has gone largely unnoticed. While some debtors have lost their battle with debt, the increasing average American income figures, combined with a finance industry which has continued to produce ever more leveraged finance products, which provide the debtor with an escape route away from the financial noose, have all combined to keep the inevitable fall at bay.

However, with the downturn of the global economy in 2008, the chickens have come home to roost!

It had to happen, because the debt spiral could not keep on climbing forever. Also, while it is toned down in media coverage, the reason why the global economy keeps on rolling backwards and forwards in a state of near brinkmanship over the last 9 years, is simply because a great amount of global debt is still unaccounted for. Until the debts have been completely worked out of the system, the global economy will continue to creek, and the US economy will continue to make progress only to stagger backwards, just when it looked like everything was back to normal again!

While this is disconcerting, the good news is that after another couple of years, the debt will be settled and the global economy will return to its normal pattern of exponential growth, at least for a little while.

Why the return to exponential growth?

Because the global economy is only moving in one direction and that's upwards!

Firstly the dynamics of a global economy allow for a rapid re-expansion of the World economy. Also, with the rise of developing economies, such as the BRIC Countries (Brazil, Russia, India and China) represent an enormous amount of people, who are rapidly increasing their standard of living!

So while global expansion obviously has its limits, for now we are far from reaching a limit of global economic capacity. Rather we are facing a bottleneck, which has been created by a banking crisis, which came about from the boom, bubble, bust of the first decade of the 21st Century!

So as soon as things settle back down again, the global economy will start moving upwards once again.

So all of this is good, right?

Yes of course, save for one thing, and that's the finance industry which has become accustomed to enormous market share and profitability. This means that within a couple of years, all the cool introductory offers will be back in town again. And sadly because of all the snug tie-ins between the finance industry and the retail industry, it is now very easy to assume debt and this is only likely to become easier over time.

And this brings us back to the 'buy today and pay back tomorrow' consumer culture. Because, what's the point in settling your credit card debts, and all of your other outstanding debts within a year, only to be back into a serious debt problem within another two to three years perhaps!

And remember that once the global economy improves, the drive of the finance industry towards ever greater levels of market penetration will result in every more enticing offers, with the intention of enticing you back into debt all over again. So with a societal financial model, which is so geared towards a debt culture, the only way to remain out of debt, once you have freed yourself from your outstanding debts, is to make a determined effort to remain in this state. Even if it means making a concerted effort to stay clear of debt, even if 5 or 6 years from now the World economy is right back into consumer debt frenzy all over again!

THE SECOND FACTOR IS DENIAL

This leads us on appropriately to the next major factor, in the resumption of credit card debt, and debt in general, and its denial.

Denial is a uniquely human trait, and it does have its uses. By the process of denial we avoid facing up to the reality of whatever it is around us, which is distasteful to our sense of self. For example, a patient maybe diagnosed with terminal cancer, and yet they ardently believe that they will be ok, even though everything indicates otherwise and a short while later they succumb to the disease!

We see other examples, such as a wealthy person, who loses their wealth overnight and yet who continues to live as before until, they are finally evicted from their house and lose all of their possessions!

These of course are extreme examples; a less extreme example might be a person who discovers that they have a serious health problem, and for a while they ignore it, until they eventually get their head around it, over time. This is extremely common! So what has happened here?

Basically the ego of the person who receives a sudden shock, such as sudden onset of ill health or financial problems for example, denies this reality. Occasionally they may completely deny the reality; however, in most cases they simply deny the reality to a certain degree. They downplay the reality of their situation!

A common example of this would be the person who suddenly loses their job and yet does not tell their family, rather they pretend to go to work every day and sit in the local library instead. While this may sound ridiculous, it's a way of coping with something which is outside of our experience. And in most cases individuals in this kind of situation will face up to the reality, although it may take them some months to do so.

So denial is a coping mechanism, and most of the time it works fairly well. It creates an internal buffer which protects the individual from the harshness of their reality, until they finally come to their senses. Occasionally, like in the case of the sick person who denies their cancer and simply sips green tea thinking that it will cure them, it can prove to be disastrous. However, more often than not , like in the case of the person who suddenly loses their job and goes about their life as if nothing happened, for a couple of months, the denial is simply a coping mechanism which will help them until they are capable of facing up to their reality.

From the point of view of debt, however, we see a far more insidious form of denial, and it is the sort of denial whereby the person who is in this state simply ignores something which is potentially hazardous over an extended period of time.

The earlier examples, of sudden onset of ill health or loss of a job, will result in the denial quickly resolving itself or in the demise of the person's health or financial wellbeing, if they chose to remain in denial. However, for people who are undergoing a far less extreme change in circumstances, it is possible to remain in denial for an extended period of time.

Examples, include the smoker who smokes 20 cigarettes a day, and who can feel some health side effects, yet they carry on regardless, quoting their uncle or aunt who smoked 50 a day and who lived to be 100! Another example, could be the obese individual who although overweight, is not morbidly so, and who also denies their situation, even tough year by year their weight increases and their health declines.

People in this kind of situation can often remain in their state of denial for decades! However, once they become cognizant of their reality, they suddenly find themselves in difficult circumstances. If the smoker has developed cancer of the bronchus, can they rewind time? Well of course not. By the same token, if the obese person has a heart attack, they too find themselves having to get on with things, and doing the best they can to make amendments. But as any doctor will tell you, prevention is always better than cure. If they could have come to their senses years ago, they would fair far better today!

The example of the individual, who ignores their health, is similar in many ways to the debtor who remains in a state of denial regarding their finances. With debt, many individuals can get by while in a state of debt, as long as it is not to extreme.

If we look at the general state of American personal finance, even ten years ago, they were too high and yet lots of people could get by. However a certain point is reached whereby the ability of the debtor to sustain the debt repayments becomes impossible. And sadly, with credit card debt, because the minimum payments are so low and the interest rates are so high, often by the time the credit card debtor realizes that they have a problem, they are already in debt to the sum of tens of thousands of dollars!

So, by way of an example, a debtor may have $1000 worth of repayment on their credit cards every month. Maybe they can cover that, but perhaps a year later they have $1500 worth of payments to make and finally they cannot cover them. Then they decide to reduce their debt, and so they take out all of their credit cards and add up all of the balances and discover that $1500 in monthly minimum payments is 2 percent of $75000!

So that's the thing with denial of debt, for a long time you can get away with it, however, when you finally face up to it, you have a colossal problem on your hands!

After a while maybe you are having trouble making payments, so you take out a new, low introductory rate credit card and transfer the debt onto this card, and so everything is ok for a while, until the introductory offer ends, and suddenly you are back to paying out lots of money each month, while making no headway with clearing the debt.

Also, if you are in a state of denial you are probably still buying things on your existing credit cards and thinking to yourself that soon, you will clear them. And of course soon never comes around, instead you simply go ever deeper into debt. Until some fine day you simply run out of new credit card options and find yourself knee deep in credit card debt. And of course most credit card debtors will usually have lots of other debts to take care of too, such as personal loans, overdraft facilities, auto loans, home loans and so on!

So, first off if you are in debt and are thinking of doing something about it, then the first step is to take a detailed look at your present lifestyle and circumstances and be very truthful to yourself. Find out just how much you owe and take a look at what way you are living your life.

That's the first thing which you must do.

Secondly, make a point of putting a stop to credit card use, at least while you are attempting to clear your debts, because, as noted earlier, so long as you use your credit cards, it is impossible to clear them. The only possible exception to this is to use one credit card which you clear each and every month. However whatever you do, do not keep on racking up credit card debts, and think to yourself that next month you will clear the debt, it simply will not get you anywhere!

Thirdly, budgeting has to become a habit, whereby at any time somebody could ask you how much you owe, and how much assets do you have and how is your monthly cash flow and you could answer them fairly accurately, of the top of your head. While this may sound extreme, it is an essential step towards getting real about your finances. After all if you are now in debt, it is because of some faulty financial actions which you took in the past. And actions always follow on from the values which we have and the level of self-awareness which we are capable off. In plain English if today you have $100,000 in debt, it didn't come about overnight. If you have $100,000 in debt today, then why did you not put a stop to it when you only had $5000 in credit card debt?

So let's go beyond excuses, I know that you probably have lots of reasons as to why you are presently in debt. However, unless you were very unfortunate, and simply ended up acquiring a huge debt over night, perhaps because of the loss of a job or ill health, than other than this genuine reason, the reality is that you made some bad decisions!

So while some credit card debtors will fall into debt, because of severe changes in circumstance, the majority fall into debt over an extended period of time as a result of many poor financial decisions, which have been ignored because they have been living in a state of denial at the time!

If this is the case with yourself, then it is time to get real and get over your state of denial. And the best way to do this is to become acutely aware of your financial reality and to start making decisions which are appropriate to your present financial reality!

Finally, getting out of credit card debt is not enough. Because you have to remain free of debt, and as we know by now, the finance industry is keen to regain their market share, and as soon as the economy Improves they will go into marketing overdrive in an attempt to regain their lost wealth. At the moment they may be laying low, in an effort to absorb their losses as best as possible, however, it's only a matter of time before they comeback full force in an effort to regain their wealth, and remember finance companies become rich by putting you and other people like you into debt!

So the only way to remain free of debt, once you have cleared your outstanding debts, is to let go of denial. While there is not much which you can do about the consumer orientated society which we live in, you can change your response to it!

There is nothing wrong with a capitalistic consumer orientated society. Nor is there anything wrong with a certain level of debt, so long as it is within reason. However, over the last 50 years, the finance industry has increasingly targeted consumers in an effort to get them to sign up to various finance agreements. And they have made many financial partnerships, with various retail outlets in an effort to increase their market share. While the market economy has many benefits, the downside is a tendency towards unbridled greed. The finance companies and the retail outlets do not care about the overall financial wellbeing of their customers, or even of the economy, they are far too engrossed in producing growth in their bottom line, than to be bothered looking at the big picture. And of course over the last 50 years, the finance companies have always made good in the long run, so why making changes to a winning formula! And this is the problem with the present era which we are living in. The balance is out the window and it has resulted in a worldwide financial collapse!

We will end up in more economic crisis all over again, and this will continue until it becomes obvious that an economy which is dependent upon the indebtedness of its citizens is not a viable long-term reality!

While I am confident that the World economy will improve, I am also confident that the finance companies and retailers, who are driven by the desire for greater profits, will continue to entice the unwary consumers back into the debt cycle. Sadly, over time we will end up in more economic crisis all over again, and this will continue until it becomes obvious that an economy which is dependent upon the indebtedness of its citizens is not a viable long-term reality!

However, this may take decades before the World at large comes to realize this simply fact, So on this level, the entire global economy is in a state of denial!

So why wait for the World to come to its senses, when you can come to you senses today?

Yes, if you are sensible and follow a good debt relief plan, you will become free of debt. However, the present economy lives on the principle of 'buy today and pay back tomorrow', so temptation will always be there. Unless you let go of your denial, unless you upgrade your financial value system, it is a forgone conclusion that sooner or later you will end up back into credit card debt all over again!

So while we cannot change the World, we can at least change our response to the World. If you want to maintain the great credit card debt escape, then it is essential that once free of debt that you remain free of it and the only way to do so is to put an end to denial and to increase your level of financial awareness. Because only by doing this can you become immune to the endless marketing spin and enticements, which are designed to get you and me and lots of people just like us back into the credit card debt spiral all over again!

The Future begins with you!

Talking about personal finances can be a scary experience. We all want to be happy and to go about our lives as we feel like. We want to live a free and undeterred existence, and often the financial stuff just gets us down!

I know only too well that in many ways it's a dog eat dog World out there, and everything which we get is hard worked for. I also know from personal experience that credit card debt is a terrible encumbrance. After all its hard enough getting on with life without having to spend the greater part of our disposable income on serving credit card debts, overdraft facilities, auto loans, home loans , personal loans and so on.

So really it is essential that we become debt free!

And while facing up to our costs may be a painful process, it is an essential one, and one which will be successful in the long term. I know from my own experience how dark and glib it can be to feel that your debts are out of control, however, I also know from my own experience that the debt can and will end if you are sensible!

So, regardless how bad it may look now, don't give up on yourself. You can do it! After all it took some years to get you into this present situation, so since it took a certain amount of time to arrive at this stage, it will usually take a certain amount of time to work things out.

If you do not like your present reality, do remember that todays present was yesterday's tomorrow and somewhere along the way you made some poor choices which resulted in your present circumstances! If you do not like your present circumstances, then simply make changes and in the future things will change. Maybe not literally tomorrow, but certainly sometime in the near future, somewhere along the timeline, not too far in the future you will be free of debt and will have better prospects!

So keep up the good work!

You have made a good start by reading this eBook, so do continue with your research, and then when you are ready to initiate a good debt relief plan, pretty soon you shall be debt free!

Free Gifts
Bonus #1 – Grab Free Books!!!!!!!!

As a way of saying thank you for downloading this book I would like to give you two free books, which are available exclusively for my readers. The free book "Juicing for Health – 35 Juicing Recipes for Everyday Health Problems", is packed full of useful healthy juice recipes and "Success Hacks - 31 Mind-Set Hacks to Increase Productivity and Career Success", is packed full of helpful mind hacks for developing a more dynamic and enjoyable lifestyle!

Go to healbodymindandspirit.com/sign-up-page/

Bonus#2 - Bonus Video Series

This video series covers many aspects of financial wellbeing and financial planning

Please go to You Tube and type in Heal Body Mind and Spirit – How to Pay off Credit Card Debts

It will bring you to my debt playlist and also my channel. There are lots of useful videos on this channel, covering all aspects of physical-mental-emotional-spiritual wellbeing and part of this of course includes things like paying off debts and how to live a good and successful life!

REVIEWS

PLEASE FEEL FREE TO POST A REVIEW. YOU CAN ACCESS MY AUTHORS PROFILE BY GOING TO WWW.AMAZON.COM THEN SELECTING BOOKS AND TYPING IN (DERMOT FARRELL – AUTHOR). THIS WILL BRING UP MY AUTHORS RPOFILE PAGE. YOU CAN THEN SELECT THIS BOOK AND WRITE A REVIEW, ALSO MY OTHER BOOKS ARE LISTED THERE

Footnotes

1. US Census Bureau credit card projections for 2012:

    Data from the US Census bureau can be found on the following website http://www.census.gov/ . Data referring to US credit card statistics and projections for the year 2012 can be found in the Census bureau document entitled 12s1188. It's a pdf table, and can be found on the following Census bureau link:

    http://www.census.gov/compendia/statab/2012/tables/12s1188.pdf

The US census bureau carries out a Census every five years. So the last Census was in 2010, and the next one will be in 2015. Consequently tables like this one (12s1188) are admittedly projections, however the US Census bureau does have a lot of resources at their disposal. Furthermore, they have no axe to grind; consequently their statistics tend to be fairly objective.

2. US population figure projections 2012:

    The US Census Bureau website has a population clock on the following we blink:

    http://www.census.gov/population/www/popclockus.html

These figures are projections, since accurate figures can only be arrived at every five years, and the next Census is not due until 2015.

The figures quoted in the text are accurate as of the time of printing of this eBook, consequently they shall vary a little from the figures on this we blink, which change on a daily basis.

The figure quoted in the text is set in the of the US Census Bureau's quick facts section which is on the following we blink:

http://quickfacts.census.gov/qfd/states/00000.html

The quick facts section states the less than 18 year age group in America represented 24% of the entire population, which suggest that the adult population accounts for the other 76% of the population. While the quick facts section quotes a population figure of just 311,591,917 (at time of publishing this ebook), this obviously differs from the population clock projections for 2012. The figures which I take as representing the US population for 2012 is set at 300,000,000, which of course is an arbitrary figure, however, it is fairly close to the actual figures at the outset of 2012, which were probably slightly greater than 300,000,000.

With this in mind I calculating that the adult population to be somewhere in the region of 23788000 people. Consequently if three are 160,000,000 credit card holders in America in 2012, the figure represents just fewer than 70% of the Adult population of America

3. Moody's April 2012 report on credit card delinquency rates:
   Moody's is one of America's biggest credit rating agencies. The produce reports throughout the year on a wide variety of financial statistics and credit ratings, not only for America but also for every Country around the World. To find out more about the statistical

information which they have on offer you can visit their website, which is http://www.moodys.com/.

4.   Federal Reserve G.19 Consumer Credit Release, November 2011.

5.   The World GDP figures per head of population in 1900 was rated at 679 international dollars (chained to 1990 levels) versus the year 2000 average GDP figures per head of population at 6539 international dollars (chained to 1990 levels), according to the preferred rating on page 5 of "**Estimates of World GDP, One Million B.C. –Present**
1998

J. Bradford De Long

Department of Economics, U.C. Berkeley

If we divide 6798 into 6539 we arrive at 9.6, which mean that the GDP per capita of World population in the year 2000 was 9.6 times greater than the per capita of World populations GDP (gross domestic product). That's practically a tenfold increase in average World wealth figures in just one Century!

Chart One – Credit Card Industry Pre Tax profits (1980 to 2007)
The data for this graph came from the report "The Effect of 2005 Bankruptcy Reform on Credit Card Industry Profits and Prices"
By Michael Simkovic
JD *cum laude*, Harvard Law School, 2007
The full text is available at http://works.bepress.com/michael_simkovic/2/

Chart Two – Median Value of Debt for Families with Holdings

The data for this graph comes from "2007 Survey of Consumer Finances Chart book", p 831.

The precise data on this graph is listed below. Please bear in mind that all figures have been chained to year 2007 figures, so when we compare 1989 debts at an average of $24,100 to 2007 average debts of $67,300, we are comparing figures in 2997 dollars!

So the jump from 1989 average household debt to 2007 average household debt is 248%!

Median Value of Debt for Families with Holdings (Data in 2007 Dollars)	
Year	$
1989	24,100
1992	24,800
1995	29,200
1998	41,400
2001	45,400
2004	60,700
2007	67,300

Chart Three – Disposable Income Compared to Credit Card Debt Chained in 2005 Dollars

The data in this chart comes from several sources. The revolving debt per household figures from 1980 to 2005 come from "Bankruptcy Reform and Credit Cards" by Michelle J. White, a working paper number 13265, from the National Bureau of Economic Research, July 2007.

The figures for 2010 are courtesy of The Federal Reserve, Consumer Credit G.19 document, which can be found at the following link:

http://www.federalreserve.gov/releases/g19/HIST/cc_hist_sa.html

The revolving credit figure for March 31st 2010 was $ 842563.18. If we divide this by the number of households in the USA as per the US 2010 Census, the household figure is 116,716,292. So this brings an average household revolving debt figure for 2010 of $16,383. When we then compare the 2005 income figures to the 2010 income figures we see a rise of just over 11%. So we factor this in to the equation which brings the 2010 revolving credit figure to $ 18,205.

Also please do note, that strictly speaking revolving credit also includes all forms of open ended credit, so not just credit cards, it also includes store cards, and home equity lines would also be considered as revolving credit. However, since credit cards account for 90% plus of the revolving credit figure, it is fair to say that revolving credit statistics present a fair figure of the state of credit card usage in the USA at any particular time!

The disposable income figures come from the Census website, www.census.gov. The document is the Table 679. "Selected Per Capita Income and Product Measures in Current and Chained (2005) Dollars". This table can be found on the www.census.gov website under the table reference 12s0679.

The figures for revolving debt in the Bankruptcy Reform paper where chained to 2006 dollar levels, whereas the figures in the selected income table are chained to 2005 dollars. To make it easier to follow, I made some calculations in order to convert the 2006 chained figures back to 2005 chained figures. Also, I used the chained figures for disposable income from the Selected Income table in order to work out conversion rates for the credit card debt, so that we could both see the actual revolving credit figures per year, as well as the revolving figures chained to 2005 rates.

While this was a cumbersome activity, I found it to be the only way to get accurate figures. While there are a great many figures bandied about the internet, many of them have either no reference to sources, or they have very ambiguous references. So, since the best way to solve a problem is to understand it, at least by attempting to come up with accurate figures, we can have some hope of arriving at a solution which will work well in the real World!

Picture Credits

Front piece

The Golden Mean between Liberty and the Guillotine

A picture depicting 19th

Century prison life

Artist unknown

Roger –Viollet Collection

The Dark Side of the Moon

Courtesy Nasa

www.nasa.com

The great Credit card Debt Escape

Anonymous prison escape drawing from the 18th

Century

outlining the daring prison escapes of Englishman jack Sheppherd, who

managed to

escape from prison 4 times before finally hanging from the end of the hangman's

noose!

Sustaining the Great Credit Card Debt Escape

This is a 1888 print, taken from the national police Gazette, of inmate Paul Honnich's daring escape from the Raymond Street jail, where he descended from the third floor via a rope made from towels!

www.ingramcontent.com/pod-product-compliance
Lightning Source LLC
Chambersburg PA
CBHW061205180526
45170CB00002B/971